366 Ways To Know Your Character

A Romance In A Month Daily Writing Workbook

Rachelle Ayala

Amiga Books

Foreword by Michele Shriver

ISBN-13: 978-1503328471

ISBN-10: 1503328473

FOREWORD by Michele Shriver

As a veteran of Rachelle Ayala's Romance in a Month class, I am thrilled to be able to present the Foreword for this exciting new Romance in a Month Workbook.

The daily character questions fast became my favorite feature of the class, as answering them always helped me learn more about my characters. In several instances, my answers made it into my book, such as the contents of my character's refrigerator.

There are different ways to use this workbook, and how it is used is up to the individual writer, but I believe it has value as a planning tool for those that are intrinsic plotters/outliners as well as writers whose style is more 'fly by the seat of their pants'.

No matter your writing style, crafting believable characters that readers can identify with and root for is an important component of any successful book, and to craft believable characters, a writer must know their characters and know them well.

This book aids you in that process by presenting questions for you to answer about your characters, from the more mundane like their favorite color to those that ask you to dig a little deeper and examine their innermost thoughts and fears.

This book can also be a quick ticket out of writer's block for those times when you might be stuck. Writer's block sometimes stems from a plot gone wrong, but it can also result from simply not knowing or understanding your characters well enough. What can you do then? Simply open this book, flip to one of the questions, and think hard about your answer. It might just tell you something you didn't know about your character and provide inspiration for that next scene!

Good luck getting to know your characters better and happy writing!

Michele Shriver writes women's fiction and contemporary romance. Her books feature flawed-but-likeable characters in real-life settings. She's not afraid to break the rules, but never stops believing in happily ever after. Michele counts among her favorite things a good glass of wine, a hockey game, and a sweet and sexy book boyfriend, not necessarily in that order.

PREFACE

Have you ever wanted ...

- To create unforgettable characters? The kind readers talk about well after the book is finished?
- Your characters to jump off the page and tell you what they like and dislike?
- To make your characters multi-dimensional, complicated, deeper, and larger than life?
- Create compelling quirks, flaws, and internal conflicts to differentiate your characters?
- To keep your story from being predictable by having your character surprise you and your reader?
- To hear readers tell you they walked with your characters, lived, loved, and felt every emotion your character experienced?
- To have an ongoing relationship with your characters so you can keep them consistent if writing a series?

366 Ways to Know Your Character is the right workbook for you. Whether you're developing your character before writing, or working it out as you're writing, answering the daily questions can stimulate your characters to surprise and shock you as well as take your story in directions you might not have expected.

Each question is designed to draw you deeper into your character's psyche. It doesn't matter whether the answer jumps out at you or that you must painfully dig it out. Either way, you will win new insights into your characters until they feel and act like real people.

DEDICATION

To the members of my
Romance In A Month
Writing Group:
You make each day of writing
a joyous one.
Thanks for coming on
this journey with me.

INTRODUCTION

366 Ways to Know Your Character is a workbook for the Romance In A Month method I devised to brainstorm and write a romance in a month's time. So far, many participants have written and published several stories in six month's time by following the process The mean time from writing to release is two to three months, giving time for revision and editing.

One of the key elements of Romance In A Month is the Daily Character Prompt which is posted every day. Participants answer the question in the thread and have fun discussing their answers with others. The writers in the group may already be writing their story or thinking about their plot. Maybe they know the answer immediately or have to think about it. The Daily Character Prompt has gotten rave reviews and many of the group members look forward to it. Their characters have oftentimes surprised them with an answer and they were able to put the answer into their story. In other cases, a completely new plotline opened up after answering the prompt.

The writers in my original Romance In A Month class have asked for a compilation of prompts, hence this book. Obviously I did not have 366 prompts while running the month long classes, but I put my creative cap on and made up enough questions to fill in an entire year plus leap day.

I hope you'll enjoy answering these questions to deepen and get to know your characters.

How to Use This Book

The print version of this book is a workbook. I have purposely given room so you can jot down your notes. You can also reuse the prompt for many novels, writing your character's name and the answer. After you are finished or have filled up the pages, this workbook would serve as a memory book for you to look back on your characters.

Please do not feel you have to use all 366 prompts for every character! To preserve the serendipity of discovering something unexpected from your character, I suggest going to today's date and filling it in for each day you are writing. Or close your eyes and pick a question at random.

The prompts alternate between using "he" and "she," however each question can apply to either gender. They are also aimed at romance, although can be adapted to any genre. Feel free to adapt and change the questions to fit your needs.

This book is for you to use any way you choose. My hope for you is that it will add another dimension to your writing and help you create fully formed characters who are memorable and intriguing.

Free free to use these prompts in your own writing group. Please check out my book, *Romance In A Month: guide to writing a romance in 30 days* for information about structuring your group or class, or join mine by looking me up in Facebook.

I'd love to hear from you.

Email me at ayala.rachelle@gmail.com with questions, suggestions, or just to share.

Happy Writing!

Your friend, Rachelle Ayala

JANUARY

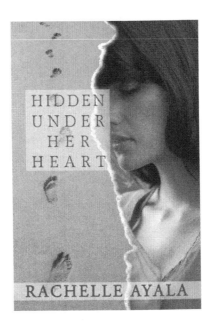

January 1
Jot down your character's New Year's Resolution List.

January 2
What is the first resolution your character breaks?

January 3

What kind of lover does your character dream about? Why? What is her current lover like?

January 4

Does your character have a deep, dark secret? What is it, and why does he not want anyone to know? Does he blame himself or someone else?

January 5

What is your character's favorite dessert? How often does she have it?

January 6

Who was your character's last relationship? How did they breakup? Are they still in touch?

January 7

What is the most embarrassing thing to happen to your character? How does it affect him today?

January 8

If your character could live anywhere in the world, where would it be and why?

January 9

What kind of person (type, occupation, age, characteristic) would your character refuse to date? Why?

January 10

What is the charity or cause your character supports? How active is she involved?

January 11

What disgusts your character?

January 12

What keeps your character up at night?

January 13
If your character won the lottery, what would he do?

January 14
Your character has met the person she thinks is the love of her life. Where is she and what is she going to do?

January 15
What does your character think is his best trait?

January 16
What dream does your character wish would come true? Is she doing anything about it or just wishing?

January 17
How does your character know he is in love?

January 18
What is your character's father like? What expectations did he have for her? How is her current relationship with him?

January 19
What is your character's most notable achievement?

January 20
What is something your character wishes she could do, but is too scared? How would she react if someone put her in the position to do that act?

January 21
What ideal does your character hold as most precious? How would he react if someone he cares about violates it?

January 22
What would your character sacrifice for love?

January 23
What does your character do to show love?

January 24
What is the last thing your character wants to do before getting married?

January 25
Does your character have pets? What type and why?

January 26
If your character can live in any historical period and place, where and when would it be?

January 27
What kind of car does your character drive? How important is it to her?

January 28
What is your character's occupation? Why did he get into that line of work? Does he enjoy it or wish he were doing something else?

January 29
Does your character have a disability or chronic illness? How does she deal with it?

January 30
Has your character ever purposely made a significant other jealous? In what circumstance? What was the outcome?

January 31
Does your character have a birthmark? How about any scars? Is he proud of them or ashamed?

FEBRUARY

February 1
Who was the last person to hurt your character deeply? What did they do?

February 2
Where does your character go or what does he do when angry? How quickly does he get over it?

February 3

What is your character's greatest fear? Has she told anyone about it? Who would she never tell and why?

February 4

What makes your character laugh out loud?

February 5

It's Saturday night. What is in your character's refrigerator? On his bedroom floor? In his garbage can? On the dashboard of his car?

February 6

What is your character's favorite book? Movie? Song? Band? TV show?

February 7

Who was your character's first love? Where is he now?

February 8

When was the last time your character cried? Why?

February 9

Does your character cook? What is her signature dish?

February 10

Does your character have any tattoos? If so, what does it mean to him?

February 11

What tech gadget can your character not live without?

February 12

Is your character a sports fan? What sport and team is her favorite?

February 13

What is your character's dream wedding? How involved is he
in planning it?

February 14

What is your character's family like? How involved are they in
her life? Does she welcome their interference or wish they
cared more?

February 15

What is something your character wish he were talented in
but is not?

February 16

What is your character's biggest regret in life? Has she dealt
with it, or is she still running?

February 17

Did your character like or dislike school? Why?

February 18
What is your character's deal breaker in a relationship? What is one thing he must have in a girlfriend?

February 19
Who is your character's best friend? How do they interact?

February 20
What is your character's worst dating experience? How did it end? Is he still seeing that person?

February 21
What is a well-meaning, but flawed, decision that your character made? How is it affecting her today?

February 22
How does your character make a decision? Does he stick to his decision or does he waver?

February 23

Does your character have a sense of style? If so, what kind of clothes does she favor? Is she conservatively dressed or likes to stand out in the crowd?

February 24

Does your character wish to be famous, rich, or powerful? If none of the above, what does he wish for most?

February 25

How does your character define success? Failure?

February 26

If your character can wish one person back to life, who would it be?

February 27

Has your character ever had a brush with death? What were the circumstances?

February 28

What is one memory your character wants to erase from her memory bank?

February 29

Is your character religious? What religion and how committed is he?

MARCH

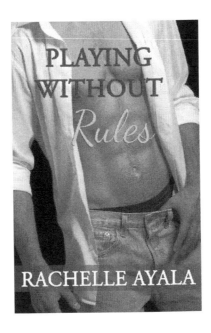

March 1
What date is your character's birthday? Does he do anything? Did his family have parties for him?

March 2
Is your character an introvert or an extrovert? What does your character wish she was? More outgoing or more introspective?

March 3

What motivates your character to get up in the morning?

March 4

Of all the people in your story, which person's death would disturb your character the most?

March 5

What is one accomplishment your character would feel he failed life if he didn't achieve it?

March 6

What is a bad habit your character has? Is she trying to quit? How is she doing?

March 7

If your character could have dinner with a public figure, who would it be? Where would they have dinner?

March 8

What is your character's dominant emotion? How does his best friend describe him?

March 9

Is your character a gossip? How does she react if her private life is revealed?

March 10

What position in the family is your character? First born, middle child, baby of the family? Only child? Does birth order make a difference in his personality?

March 11

Who is your character's favorite grandparent? Which side of the family and why?

March 12

Does your character like to travel or is he a homebody?

March 13

What is an emotional blind spot for your character? Which person in her life reminds her to watch for it?

March 14

Does your character like animals? What is his favorite animal?

March 15

What kind of games does your character play? Video games, card games, brainteasers, board games? How competitive is your character? Does she play to win or for companionship?

March 16

What is your character's relationship with his mother like? How was it growing up? How are they now?

March 17

Is your character a team player or a loner? How does that affect her relationship with her coworkers?

March 18
Does your character worry about body image? Has he done anything about it?

March 19
Did your character ever join a fraternity or sorority or is he/she against that type of forced conformity?

March 20
Does your character play a musical instrument or wish he played one?

March 21
Has your character ever been a groupie or devoted fan of a band or performing artist? Has she ever acted on the fantasy?

March 22
What does your character feel guilty about? Is he trying to make amends or burying it deep?

March 23

Has your character ever run away from home? When and why? What was the outcome?

March 24

Is your character good in sports? If so, what sport? If not, what sport does he fantasize he is good at?

March 25

Has your character ever had a crush on a teacher or professor? Did he act on it?

March 26

Has your character ever broken a law? What was the most serious law your character broke and what was the circumstance? Did she think she was morally justified?

March 27

Does your character own a gun? What does he use the gun for?

March 28

How honest is your character? Does she tell white lies? Is she a compulsive liar? Or does she think she never lies?

March 29

How is your character doing financially? Does he budget for purchases or bounce checks? Does he save for a rainy day or lives from check to check?

March 30

Does your character keep up with her ex-boyfriends or does she cut them off? Is there one she wishes she kept in touch with or one she wishes she'd never see again?

March 31

What kind of music does your character like?

April 1

How is your character's sense of humor? Does she clown
around or is she the serious type? How does she react to
someone playing a prank on her? Is she a prankster? What
was an epic prank she played and what was the
consequence?

April 2

Did your character ever cheat on an exam? Was he caught?
Why did he do it?

April 3

Did your character have to work while going to school? What was her job?

April 4

How does your character treat his younger sister, if he has one? Younger brother? Or younger cousins?

April 5

How does your character view people who are not as financially well of as he?

April 6

Does your character pray or does she handle things herself? Who does she turn to if she needs help?

April 7

Has your character ever had a broken heart? Who caused it and is he over it?

April 8

Does your character like to read? How many books does she read a month? What genres?

April 9

Is your character a hard worker or does he like to take it easy and have fun?

April 10

How humble would your character's friends say she is? Is it false modesty?

April 11

What is your character's greatest pleasure? How often does he seek it?

April 12

How responsible is your character? Is she punctual? Does she return things she borrowed?

April 13
Is your character strong and powerful or fast and agile? What is his body type?

April 14
What is considered a good day for your character? A bad day?

April 15
Has your character ever had to confess to a crime or a misdeed he did not do? What made him confess?

April 16
Does your character meditate? Why does she meditate if she does? Does she fast? Is it religious or for health reasons?

April 17
If your character could be king for a day, which country would he rule and what would he do?

April 18

Has your character ever saved anyone's life? Describe what
   happened.

April 19

Is your character attracted to someone who is her opposite? Is
   she a risk taker in love or does she prefer to play it safe?

April 20

Does your character like to garden or work on a farm? Does he
   enjoy nature? How would he react if he lost all of his
   electronic gadgets and had to live in the woods for a
   month?

April 21

Does your character prefer to date within her league, or does
   she want a man way above her in social status, looks,
   influence, or does she play it safe with guys who are below
   her on the social scale?

April 22

How patient is your character? Does she get annoyed by
traffic, cutting in and out of lanes, or does she go with the
flow? How about waiting for something she wants?

April 23

How well has your character kept himself from getting hurt by
affairs of the heart? Has he ever gone after a woman who
was clearly unavailable or who clearly hated him?

April 24

Has your character ever seen a ghost? Does she believe in
ghosts? What would she do if she had to spend the night
alone in a house where someone was murdered?

April 25

Does your character watch TV alone or with others? What
types of shows does he watch?

April 26
How well does your character accept herself? Is she always seeking to improve herself? Does she take care of her health and appearance?

April 27
Does your character like to tweak people and play the devil's advocate? Who was the last person he pissed off when he expressed an opinion contrary to consensus?

April 28
Does your character keep promises? Can her friends rely on her to do what she says? What is one promise your character should have kept but broke?

April 29
Do people go to your character for advice or do they always give him advice? How much wisdom does your character have? Common sense or book knowledge?

April 30
What is her character's favorite sexual position? Why?

MAY

May 1
Is your character a contentious person or peaceful? Does she pick her battles or shies away from conflict?

May 2
How vengeful is your character? Does he forgive easily or does he seek to do damage to someone who wrongs him? What if it were someone who hurt the woman he loves? How far would he go to extract his pound of flesh?

May 3

Is your character a rule follower or a rule breaker? Give an
example of a situation where she followed or broke a rule
and it backfired.

May 4

What is your character's comfort food? Who cooked it for him
and what does it remind him of?

May 5

Is your character afraid of blood or does she love blood and
guts? Is she squeamish about touching dead things? How
about her own blood? Needles?

May 6

Is there a person who your character is absolutely, one
hundred percent sure loves him? Who is it, and how did
that person affect him?

May 7

Was your character an obedient child or one who got into
trouble a lot? How has that carried into her adult life?

May 8

Does your character give more than receive? Is there a person in your character's life who gives more to him? A person who takes more of him?

May 9

How much does your character value privacy? Does she post everything she does on the internet? Or does she keep her activities to herself?

May 10

Has your character ever been to court? Was he the defendant or was he on the witness stand?

May 11

When was the last time your character got really drunk? Who was she with? What did she do?

May 12

Does your character have an enemy? Who is it and what is he doing about this person?

May 13
Does your character volunteer to serve in the community? Where and why does she do it?

May 14
Has your character suffered from a disease, injury, emotional disturbance, hunger, abuse, or physical deprivation? What was it and how did it shape his personality and outlook to life?

May 15
Does your character take pains to improve her physical appearance or is she more interested in her inner self? Does she read self-help books or attend seminars? Of what type?

May 16
Is your character a show-off or is he shy? Was he admired in school or did he get picked on?

May 17

Who does your character bicker and fight with most in her life? Sister, best friend, mother, boyfriend, father, child, stranger, boss, etc.?

May 18

Does your character have any hobbies? What is one hobby he would not give up even if his girlfriend or wife requested him to quit?

May 19

Has your character ever committed vandalism? What was the act, when, and was she caught? What did she have to do for restitution?

May 20

If there is one thing your character would want to change about his significant other, what would it be? What if in order to get that change, he would have to change something of his own at her request?

May 21

Has your character ever been in an accident before? Was she injured? Does she suffer from post traumatic stress over it?

May 22

Does your character easily believe what other people tell him or does he weigh all the evidence before deciding whether to believe someone? Does he check out someone's story or gives people the benefit of doubt? Has he ever been taken advantaged of?

May 23

Who does your character blame when things go wrong?

May 24

If your character is a bone marrow match to a person who has hurt her family deeply, let's say a drunk driver who killed a family member or a rapist who raped and killed someone she loves, would she donate? Why or why not?

May 25

What was your character's favorite subject in school? What subject did he wish he was good at?

May 26

If your character knew a coworker was embezzling from the company, would she report him? What if her company were endangering the health of the community? Would she blow the whistle? What would she fear?

May 27

What is your character's prized possession? Under what condition would he sell it or give it up?

May 28

Is your character a powerful public speaker or is she afraid to speak in front of an audience?

May 29

Would your character go on a blind date alone? Has he ever tried online dating?

May 30

What club or organization has your character tried to join and
has gotten rejected from? Was she disappointed,
resentful, or vowed to try again?

May 31

Who is your character most envious of? What does he wish he
had? If he were given the opportunity to trade places with
this person, would he do it?

JUNE

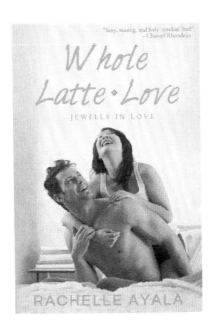

June 1
Is your character quick to anger or does she burn slowly?

June 2
What is your character's worst nightmare? Is there a possibility it could come true? If so, what does your character do to avoid it?

June 3

Do your character's parents have a happy marriage or one
filled with contention? Or did your character grow up in a
single parent home or with no parents?

June 4

If your character could take on another identity and go out on
the town with no consequences, what would she do and
where would she go?

June 5

Has your character ever stalked an ex-girlfriend? Did he get
caught? If not, how did he get over her?

June 6

Has your character ever stripped in front of people? Did she
enjoy their reactions or was she shy? Was she drunk?
What happened?

June 7

Is your character impressed by money, fame, and position?
Does he curry favor with those whose social status is

above him? Would he pretend to be someone he isn't to fit into a country club?

June 8
Who was one person your character hurt and regrets. What has she done to make amends?

June 9
Did your character believe in Santa Claus and the tooth fairy when he was young?

June 10
How important is money in your character's life? Does she use money to measure success? How does money stack up against other more nebulous things like happiness or love?

June 11
What kind of person is most wrong for your character yet tempts him the most? How does he resist?

June 12

Is your character susceptible to flattery? Is her self-esteem
dependent on what other people think about her?

June 13

Does your character prefer to live alone or with a large family?
Did he grow up in the vicinity of a large extended family
or in a small nuclear family? What if his significant other
grew up in the opposite type of family as his own? How
well do you think he'll adjust?

June 14

Under what circumstances will your character be able to
forgive his lover or wife cheating on him? What would
that person have to do to win him back, if it is even
possible?

June 15

What is one forbidden thing your character craves? Is it a
secret addiction or do all of her friends know about it?
Does she ask for help or try to resist alone?

June 16

Is your character a loud, boisterous person who prefers to be the center of attention or a quiet one who likes to remain in the background? Which does he prefer in a life partner?

June 17

What is your character's attitude toward those who are stuck up or proud? Does he admire them for achieving their position or does he want to take them down a peg?

June 18

What would your character do if she found out someone close to her betrayed her? Maybe it's a secret, or stealing from her, or having sex with her boyfriend or husband?

June 19

Has your character ever been in jail or locked up? How about imprisoned as a prisoner of war or in a concentration camp?

June 20

How well does your character sleep? Does she fall asleep as
   soon as her head hits the pillow or do worries nag at her?
   Does she use sleeping aids?

June 21

Be truthful. Is there any group of people that your character is
   prejudiced against? Is it race, culture, religion, sexual
   orientation, status, or something else? How does he hide
   it or does he not care?

June 22

Was there something your character was blamed for that she
   was innocent? Is she the one who looks guilty or can she
   brazenly shift blame to someone else? If she has, does she
   feel guilty about it?

June 23

Has your character ever seriously wished he were dead? Did
   he do anything about it?

June 24

Is there someone your character has cut out of her life completely? What was the provocation? Does she sometimes wish she could reconcile with that person?

June 25

How well does your character react to stress? Is he able to keep his cool or does he explode? Under what conditions would he freak out? Is there a talisman or mantra that helps him stay calm?

June 26

How nosy and bossy is your character? Is she always trying to fix other people's problems? Does she butt into other people's business so she can avoid facing her own problems? Do the people around her welcome her input or do they resent her?

June 27

Does your character enjoy being around children? What if they are noisy and rambunctious? Does he feel at ease with babies or does he want to escape?

June 28

What is a sexual fantasy your character has told no one about?

June 29

Does your character turn the other cheek when someone wrongs him or does he seek revenge? Does he consider it a weakness to let someone get the better of him? What about if that person hurt someone he loves?

June 30

How much time does your character spend organizing her life? Does she make lists? How does she react when someone disrupts her schedule?

JULY

July 1
If your character knew that her best friend's boyfriend or
husband were having an affair, would she tell her friend,
warn the cheater to stop, or stay silent?

July 2
Has your character ever desired his brother's girlfriend? Did
he do anything about it? What if she flirts with him?
Would he act on it?

July 3

Your character's date is a daredevil and has given her a choice of the following activities: sky-diving, rappelling off a skyscraper, bungee-jumping, pole-dancing at a strip club, singing the Star Spangled Banner at the World Series. Which one would she do?

July 4

Your character is asked to impersonate a dead rock star for a charity event. Which rock star would he impersonate and what song would he sing?

July 5

Who would your character jump into shark infested water to save?

July 6

If there were two people your character could fix up and be guaranteed they'd fall in love with each other, who would it be? (This question excludes your character as one of the two people).

July 7

What is something your character asked for and never received? How old was he?

July 8

Does your character snoop her husband or boyfriend's email, text messages and whereabouts? If she does, why does she do that? What would she do if she found something incriminating? Would she confront him or do something to undermine him?

July 9

Has your character ever caused someone's death? What was the circumstance? Does the guilt still bother him?

July 10

Would your character rather be homeless than prostitute herself? What if she had dependent children?

July 11

Has your character ever seen a therapist? What was it for? Did it help?

July 12

If your character were given a chance for free plastic surgery, would she take it? What procedure would she get done?

July 13

Has your character ever taken home a stray animal? What was it and did the animal live or die?

July 14

When and how did your character lose his virginity?

July 15

Does your character like horror movies? What is her favorite horror movie? If she's afraid of them, which one scares her the most? Would she date a guy who insisted she watch horror movies with him? What would she extract in exchange if she does?

July 16

Is your character a neat freak or is he messy? Does he rely on others to pick up after him? What if he met someone who was messier than he? Would he clean up after her or walk out?

July 17
Where would your character's dream honeymoon be? What activities would she want to include?

July 18
If your character lost all his money, what would he do first? Who would he go to?

July 19
Does your character prefer to live in the city, suburbs, country or wilderness? What happens if she meets the man of her dreams and he prefers the opposite?

July 20
Has your character ever had an affair with a married person? Was he caught by the husband? What happened?

July 21

Has your character ever had an unwanted pregnancy or been the cause of an unwanted pregnancy? What were some of the decisions she made?

July 22

What if your character found out he was the result of an unwanted pregnancy or that his mother tried to abort him? How would he feel differently about himself? Would he confront his mother?

July 23

Has your character ever been a servant or maid? Has she done things she is not proud of because her employer asked her to?

July 24

What type of house does your character dream of? What is the architectural style? Where would it be? Would he build it himself, design it, or buy it premade?

July 25

Has your character ever sacrificed her own happiness for a loved one? Did she give up something she wanted to do to take care of someone else? What did she do and how long was her sacrifice?

July 26

Has your character ever traced his genealogy? How important is family to him? Does he keep in touch with members of his extended family or clan?

July 27

Has your character ever pretended to love someone? What was the circumstance? Did she feel guilty for fooling the other person?

July 28

How does your character decide who to be friends with? Does he seek out friends or hangs out with those who are convenient? Does he have a lot of casual acquaintances or one or two very close friends?

July 29

Has your character ever had to be the bearer of bad news?
What was it and how did the experience affect her?

July 30

Has your character ever witnessed a crime? Did he get
involved? Did it put him in danger? What happened?

July 31

Does your character believe in miracles? Has a miracle ever
happened to her or someone she knows?

AUGUST

August 1
Has your character ever been abused by a parent or relative? How did he deal with it? Does he fear he will grow up to be an abuser?

August 2
Has your character ever framed someone for something she did? Was she caught? Did she feel guilty when the other person took her punishment? What if the other person found out later that she was the culprit?

August 3

What is something romantic your character would do on a first date? What is her dream date?

August 4

Which relative does your character dread a visit from?

August 5

What was your character's childhood like? Was he pampered, overprotected, or left on his own? Did he wish his parents were someone else?

August 6

What type of death does your character fear? If she had her choice what would she want to die from? (do not choose die in her sleep).

August 7

What heinous crime does your character believe is unforgivable? What if this crime is committed by someone he is in love with? Will he turn against her or try to understand?

August 8
If your character could sabotage a rival's career without repercussion, would he do it? Under what conditions would he rationalize that it would be the right thing to do?

August 9
Who would your character give all her money and possessions to help out? What if she knew it would leave her to a lonely life of perpetual poverty, i.e. no fairy tale endings?

August 10
If your character had to lose a friend forever in exchange for success in his chosen field, a scientific breakthrough that saved many lives, would he do it?

August 11
Does your character believe in dreams come true, happy endings, and true love? If yes, what would persuade her to give up her beliefs. If no, what would it take to change her mind?

August 12

How long will your character put up with a homeless friend camping on his couch? What if the friend were plain lazy? What would he do to get rid of the leech?

August 13

Would your character ever check out of life, i.e. join a commune, a convent, become a monk, or take off traveling alone? What would cause him to do so? What would cause him to come back to society?

August 14

If your character could instantly get anyone in the world to fall in love with her, who would it be? Do not list the hero of your story. Instead think about a person who really exists in history or present day.

August 15

Does your character believe in ghosts? Has he had any paranormal encounters?

August 16
How long would your character wait for a husband or lover who was missing and declared dead? What would she do if she were to finally find new love and the person she thought was dead were to reappear?

August 17
To what lengths would your character do to find a child he sired with a woman he did not love? What would he do when he finds the child?

August 18
What would your character do if she found out her parents lied or interfered in a way that caused her to break up with the man she loves?

August 19
What would your character do if his lover or girlfriend suffered amnesia and does not remember anything about him. What if she was told he had caused her accident and refuses to believe they had been in love?

August 20

Who is your character closer to, her real sisters or friends she has more in common with? What if her real sisters disapprove of her friends?

August 21

Has your character ever beaten someone up really badly? Was it justified? If so, would he do it again?

August 22

Has your character ever succumbed to peer pressure and stole something or took drugs or played a prank? Did any repercussions happen?

August 23

What types of books are on your character's e-reader that he would never admit to reading?

August 24

Was your character a favored child or was she jealous of another sibling? What did that sibling get that she did not? Why does she think her parents treated them differently?

August 25

Did your character fail to get his dream job or career? If so, what has he had to take instead? Did he give up or channel his energies into something he could do better?

August 26

Would your character dress to conform to her crowd of friends or associates or would she stick out with her own style?

August 27

What is more attractive to your character? A person who is opposite to his values, beliefs, and out of his comfort zone, or a person he is compatible with and sees eye to eye with?

August 28

What does your character think when bad things happen to good people? What are her beliefs about why these things happen?

August 29

How does your character handle loneliness? What if he were to lose all his friends because of a stand he took?

August 30

How well does your character persuade other people to do what she wants them to do? Is she the leader of her social group, work group, or family? Or does she wait for someone else to take charge? How comfortable is she when she has to make a tough decision?

August 31

What belief system is your character vehemently against? What does he do when he meets people with that belief? What if his daughter or sister were to date someone with that belief?

SEPTEMBER

September 1
Does your character want children? How many? Where would he want to raise them? City, country, location?

September 2
Does your character have a mentor at work? Who is it and how influential is this person? What if this person disapproved of your character's choice for a mate?

September 3

What is your character's favorite color? What does that color
   signify to her?

September 4

Would your character rather cling to life in ignominy and
   shame or die a noble death? What if there were children
   dependent on him?

September 5

How does your character get along with her mother? What is
   her mother like? Do they have the same taste in men or
   are they attracted to polar opposites?

September 6

Does your character put himself first or does he nurture
   someone else? Does he pin his hopes and dreams on a
   relationship or his own accomplishments?

September 7

What is your character's love language? Does he give gifts, say
   nice words, do nice things, pay special attention, or give

physical affection? What is the love language of his partner and how does it match or cause conflict in their relationship?

September 8
Does your character speak her mind and rebuke other people when they're wrong, or does she stay quiet and let things slide? Does this trait cause conflict with other characters?

September 9
Where does your character go when he's been hurt? Does he go to a mountain cabin to get away or take off on an adventure vacation? Or does he bury himself in work?

September 10
What would your character's former teachers say about her? Did your character live up to her potential, do something different or exceeded expectations?

September 11
Would your character accept a child that was the product of adultery or cheating? Would he or she forgive the partner

who cheated for the sake of the child? What if the partner who cheated left them with the child?

September 12

Has your character ever withheld important information from his or her partner? If so, what is it and what happened when the partner found out?

September 13

Does your character keep a diary or journal? What would be the most damning thing in that diary? What would happen if their lover were to read it?

September 14

Does your character believe in love at first sight? Has that every happened to him? What did he do about it?

September 15

Has your character ever been left at the altar? How did that experience change her perspective on love?

September 16

Did your character take a vow that interferes with his love life? How did he deal with the conflict between the vow and what his lover wants or needs?

September 17

What socio-economic background did your character come from? In what circles is she most comfortable with? What will she do if she is attracted to a guy from the other side of the spectrum as she is?

September 18

Does your character carry a weapon? If so, what kind? Has he ever had to use it? If he doesn't carry a weapon what does he rely on?

September 19

Does your character prefer a lover who is in a safe profession with a stable lifestyle or one who is exposed to danger and has an exciting lifestyle?

September 20

Has your character ever had a one night stand? Did he regret it? Did the casual one night stand backfire, i.e. accidental pregnancy? Woman turned into a crazy stalker? Social disease?

September 21

Has your character ever dressed up in a costume and had sex while in character? What was the costume and character? How did the other person respond?

September 22

How does your character relate to her neighbors? Is she buddies with them or does she keep them at a distance? Are there any neighbors she has a feud with? Over what?

September 23

Does your character have a healthy self-esteem or are there issues that have kept her down on herself? Was she bullied as a child or is there a flaw that makes her feel she is not good enough?

September 24

What would your character do if he were maimed, i.e. lose his arm, leg, hands? Would he allow his partner to take care of him? Or would he push her away because she deserved a better man?

September 25

If your character were offered the wealth of the entire world for the life of a single child, one she was not related to and suffered from a disease, which would she choose? Would she regret her choice? What if it were the life of the man she loves? For example, he jumps in the ocean to save a juvenile delinquent?

September 26

Has your character done something he thinks is unforgivable? If so, what is it, and what would he do to clean his slate?

September 27

Has your character ever had to admit to a serious mistake? Did she come forward on her own or was it dragged out of her?

September 28
Does your character believe in second chances? Would he take back an ex-wife? What if she'd committed a crime and was jailed? Would he wait for her?

September 29
Did your character have to overcome any childhood issues such as stuttering, learning disability, physical difficulties? How did it make her stronger?

September 30
Did your character date a lot in high school and college? Was she popular or a late bloomer?

OCTOBER

October 1
Did your character have a sibling who died young? What happened and how did it affect him growing up?

October 2
Is your character embarrassed about her family member? Who is it and what is the cause? What does she hope to do about it?

October 3

Does your character like to get his picture taken? Does he like looking at himself in the mirror or does he avoid it? How often does he post pictures of himself in social media?

October 4

What kind of in-laws do your character prefer? Large, nosy family or ones who leave well alone? Does your character expect to make friends with his or her in-laws?

October 5

Does your character defer gratification? Or does he want to live it up now that he has succeeded? Does he regret not doing things when he was younger or is he glad he did not paint the town red?

October 6

How artistic is your character? Does she enjoy visual arts? Does she decorate her home with art pieces? Love to go to galleries? Does she do crafts?

October 7

Does your character want to marry at a young age or an older age? What age does your character see as the ideal age to get married?

October 8

Does your character want to maintain a separate checkbook after she is married? Will she take her husband's name? Or does she want to retain some of her own identity, her own accounts and friends?

October 9

Has your character ever gone hunting? Killed or shot an animal? How about fishing?

October 10

Has your character ever gone to Vegas or been gambling? What was their favorite game of chance? Did she walk away while ahead or end up losing everything she won?

October 11
Has your character ever been the best man or maid of honor at a wedding? How did the dance between the best man and maid of honor go?

October 12
Does your character prefer skiing and snowboarding over surfing and boogie boarding? Or are they equally at home on the slope and the beach?

October 13
Name a location your character fantasizes about making love at.

October 14
What was your character's greatest victory? Was it a sporting event? A musical competition? A beauty contest? Or an academic achievement?

October 15
Is your character in competition with a brother or sister for an achievement? For example, both are in the same sport, or

both are trying out for cheerleading and only one can win. How did he or she handle it?

October 16

Does your character anticipate being a stepparent? If not, is it something that will be a struggle? What if the child hates your character?

October 17

Is there a family ritual your character enjoys? Some custom that is always done? What if it were something his lover disliked? Would he give it up for her?

October 18

Would your character prefer high brow entertainment, opera, symphony or museum tour over monster truck rally or rodeo?

October 19

If your character could make a pilgrimage, where and who would they go to see?

October 20

If your character could live in a famous person's house for a week, whose house would they choose?

October 21

If your character could be granted a special power, what would it be?

October 22

If your character could attend any university in the world free of charge, which one would he choose and what would he study, assuming he didn't have to worry about finding a job afterward?

October 23

Has your character ever been a teacher or taught before? Who was her most memorable student?

October 24

Does your character have friends from childhood that she keeps in touch with?

October 25

Is your character a member of a club or organization? Does he attend regular meetings, is an officer, or just hangs in the fringes?

October 26

Is your character more interested in sleeping with a lot of people, or finding the one person who is his or her soul mate? Does he or she believe there is one person destined by fate or that there are a number of people who can end up as his or her mate?

October 27

Has your character ever heard voices? Under what condition?

October 28

How important is the physical body to your character? Will she refuse to date someone who is not her desired body type? Or is personality more important?

October 29

Has your character ever destroyed another person's relationship? How? Did he regret it or would do it all over again?

October 30

Does your character hold grudges? Does he delight in paying someone back for something done wrong? How long does your character remember bad deeds?

October 31

What did your character want to be while growing up and what did he end up as a career?

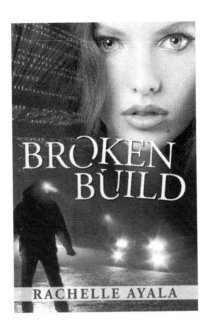

November 1

Does your character consider herself inhibited or uninhibited? What would her best friends say? What does her boyfriend or husband wish?

November 2

Does your character believe he is good in bed? Does he secretly suspect his bed partners are faking or is he confident he has given them a good time?

November 3

Has your character ever had a friend who was a very bad influence on her? Did she stick to this friend even after it was proven that the friend did not have her best interests at heart?

November 4

What is a trait that your character believes is positive about himself, but others see as negative? How does this cause conflict in his relationships?

November 5

Does your character like surprises or do surprises unsettle her? Does she peek at the ending when reading mysteries? Sneak into the closet to look at Christmas presents?

November 6

How good is your character at keeping secrets? Can she be trusted with the deadliest of secrets or does she blurt out at the worst moment?

November 7
Has your character ever had a secret crush on someone? Who was it? Why were they unattainable?

November 8
Has your character ever followed a calling? Believed that his life was meant to go a certain way?

November 9
Does your character view herself as average and normal or did she believe she is special and extraordinary? Does she try to blend in or stand out?

November 10
How important is family loyalty to your character? Would he give up someone he loved for his family?

November 11
If your character was unable to have children naturally would she adopt? Would she adopt a child of a different race or ethnicity? How would she respond to outside criticisms?

November 12

Has your character ever led a rebellion against authority? Was the rebellion justified?

November 13

Does your character wish he was someone else? Who and why?

November 14

Does your character believe in capital punishment? Under what circumstances?

November 15

Has your character ever dated someone outside of her ethnic or cultural group? Would she if given the opportunity? Is there an ethnic or cultural group she would refuse to date?

November 16

Has your character ever suffered from depression or anxiety? What has helped?

November 17

Does your character get homesick for his childhood home? What gets him nostalgic?

November 18

Has your character ever been in a gang? What was the gang like? Was it criminal or social?

November 19

What is something true that your character never had the heart to tell a loved one? Was it to avoid hurting feelings or to avoid confrontation?

November 20

What is your characters feeling toward the police? Does she believe they are there to protect or to oppress?

November 21

Is your character a veteran or has veterans in his or her family? How has war affected the family?

November 22

What is your character grateful for?

November 23

Would your character rather have many sexual partners or many caring relatives?

November 24

Does your character enjoy shopping? Does she like to shop physically or online? Does she go alone or with friends?

November 25

What do you think your character is doing while no one is watching? Would he be embarrassed to be caught?

November 26

What is one big event your character is looking forward to?

November 27

What does your character do to relax? What are some of his favorite recreational activities?

November 28

Has your character ever taken naked selfies? Has he or she sent them to someone else or posted them?

November 29

Does your character's family have any feuds against another family? How long has it been going on? How did it start?

November 30

Has your character ever slept with his or her boss? What was the outcome?

DECEMBER

December 1

Does your character collect anything? What is it? Is it valuable or whimsy?

December 2

Has your character ever gone on a program or to a retreat to improve herself? Has she ever been to rehab?

December 3
Is your character optimistic or pessimistic about the future of the world? Does he keep up with current events?

December 4
Would your character rather die young and pretty and be mourned, or outlive all the people she knows and die alone?

December 5
Does your character sing well? Does he sing to audiences or only in his shower? Or is he unable to carry a tune?

December 6
Has your character ever stabbed someone in the back to get a promotion or climb over them up the ladder at work? Did she regret it later?

December 7
Has your character ever wished he or she were a single parent so he or she can make all the decisions for a child without interference?

December 8

Does your character prefer to be in control of all aspects of her life or would she rather someone else figured things out for her?

December 9

What is your character's greatest strength? His greatest weakness? Would his self-assessment agree with that of his employer? Parents? Significant other? Friends?

December 10

For who does your character still mourn for after all these years?

December 11

For what cause would your character willingly sacrifice his life?

December 12

Has your character ever agreed to marry someone she wasn't fully in love with? Did she agree out of duty, embarrassment, settling, or necessity?

December 13

How important are the holidays for your character? How much does she decorate? What does she look forward to? Family get together? Gifts? Parties? Or seasonal cheer?

December 14

What would your character want to leave a lasting legacy as? Is it an accomplishment? Children? Fame? Having made the world a better place?

December 15

How important is patriotism to your character?

December 16

What is something your character did that she is ashamed of?

December 17

Does your character have any heroes or people he admires? Who?

December 18
What is something your character wants most in life?

December 19
Does your character have a past she wants to get away from? What is it that she did? Or is it a person?

December 20
Where does your character see himself in five years? Ten? What does he imagine is eulogy will say?

December 21
Are there any rules your character lives by? How does she feel if she breaks one of her own rules?

December 22
What kind of parenting style does your character have? Is she lenient and indulgent? Strict and firm? Or tries to be a friend?

December 23
Which parent did your character prefer when growing up? Mom or Dad? And why?

December 24
What does your character usually do on Christmas Eve?

December 25
What does your character want for Christmas? Describe a typical Christmas at his or her home.

December 26
Does your character keep gifts he doesn't like but treasure them for the person who sent it, or does he rush to the store to exchange it?

December 27
If your character were to find herself widowed or divorced, would she remain single or try to find another man?

December 28

What is your character like in the face of danger? Who would
   he protect?

December 29

How attractive does your character consider herself? What is
   her most desirable feature? Least desirable? Does she
   flaunt what she has?

December 30

What is your character's overall self-esteem? Does he feel
   worthy of being loved? Does he feel competent at his job?

December 31

How does your character spend New Year's Eve? Does she
   attend a large party? Stay home with family and close
   friends? Go to bed early or countdown at midnight? Does
   she always have to have someone to kiss at the stroke of
   midnight?

Review Quotes About Rachelle Ayala's Characters

Michal's Window

"We get to walk, run, fear, and most importantly, love as Michal does."

"If you like your heroes and villains simple and uncomplicated, this is not a book for you."

"For weeks I was immersed ... by legendary people so alive and lively I felt like I'd met them for real."

"Her dealing with human nature is superb."

"Her character development is simply AWESOME."

"Character development - 5 points - you definitely get to know the characters in this book."

"... characters that you can't help but to love them or hate them."

Broken Build

"I enjoyed Jen. Now there's a woman who has everything--a great body, a great job and a several damaging secrets!"

"Dave is a unique main character. He's quite tortured and not afraid to show it--at least not after he feels like he can let his guard down around Jen."

"Jen Jones is a character that I had a love/hate relationship with throughout the book."

"The thing that held my interest most of all was Jen. I always long for a strong female character and am often disappointed. The story line is technical computer savvy wit that even I understood and I'm far from being a computer whiz!"

"She is a very realistic woman, and even though I wanted to slap her a few times, lol, I found her totally adorable."

"The main male character had just the right mix of strong and sexy/yet tragic and vulnerable to drive me crazy!"

Whole Latte Love

"I liked the characters a lot, I loved Dylan (he is my sweetheart now)."

"This book had me captivated. Dylan and Carina had me going a little cray-cray at one point."

"He wins your heart without really trying."

"Her goody-two shoes attitude and constantly ruining the moment drove me mad! But hey, it's good when an author can get a character to make you feel real emotions."

"She will have you laughing, gasping, sometimes even have you shaking your head at how you can actually picture things happening in real life."

"The entire thing was brought together by two very realistic, very human main characters in Carina and Dylan. They both have passions, flaws, and make mistakes, some of them endearing, some of them making you want to shake them and ask what they were thinking."

"The character development, not only of the two whose lives we follow in Carina and Dylan, but in the many supporting roles seen in their friends, family, and co-workers, helps set this book apart from so many mass market paperback romance novels that are too busy spending time with hot steamy sex scenes to bother giving the characters personality."

"Ayala produced an enchanting and thoroughly captivating plot - moving at a fantastic pace – with smoking hot characters who are realistic and easy to love."

"A fantastic read, this book will tug the right strings in your heart. Most probably, all of them!"

Hidden Under Her Heart

"A story that takes the reader up and down the emotional scales in the lives of Maryanne and Lucas."

"We have some really smarmy characters that you are going to love to hate!"

"In a flash, I was so absorbed with the story that I found myself caring about what happened to the characters."

"Very rarely do I find myself crying over a book, but this one brought me to literal tears."

"The hero, Lucas, was my favorite. He started off great and he had me rolling! He's upbeat and hilarious at opportune times, but straight forward and serious, letting his voice shine when it all boils down to his compassion for life."

"My favorite part about Lucas was the growth his character took in the book."

Knowing Vera

"And Vera. I totally loved that girl! I want to say she's my favorite out of the three books, but I can't because Jen was an equally favorite."

"I'm amazed that the author of *Knowing Vera* also write *Michal's Window* and *Hidden Under Her Heart*. Both of those earlier works are superb examples of her range in writing fiction that compels the reader to love the main characters, flaws and all."

"Vera has a great voice and I just loved the way she looks at things and her determination. Zach is totally swoon-worthy and a great hero who will capture your heart."

"Their characters grow throughout the story and as readers we get to know them practically at a personal level."

"The first thing that really jumped out at me about this book is Vera's distinctive voice."

"Vera is a girl everyone would love to fall in love with. Zach on the other hand is not only an eye-candy; he has a heart to match his features."

Taming Romeo

"Rachelle Ayala knows how to write a book that will make you laugh, then cry then laugh once again! She truly can make you feel what the characters are feeling—from me—this gets a 10!!"

"I really loved how detailed and realistic the characters and setting were, it's easy to see that the author truly put for an amazing effort to keep this book romantic, humorous and realistic."

Claiming Carlos

"Rachelle Ayala is a master at creating and transforming an intense connection between the reader and her incredible characters. You find yourself not just cheering them on in reaching their goals, but you rejoice in their successes, and ultimately have your heart ripped out when their world falls apart. Once the journey ends, you will find that you are emotionally drained as you quiet literally experienced the story in the same way that the characters did."

"What is remarkable about the book is that neither the characters, nor their words are shallow at any point—the author doesn't make light of any situation in the book or brushes it off with cliché sentences. Instead she has carefully carved out the emotional dynamics in the different scenes throughout and the dialogues, thoughts and language are all used in sync with this."

"The characters are well built and I especially love Carlos. In fact, it's quite hard for a girl not to fall for Ayala's heroes, (I fell in the same way for Romeo and Dylan in her previous books)."

"What this author seems to have is a great knack for creating down-to-earth-believable-characters, the kind readers tend to invest serious time in, losing themselves in the characters' problems and struggles."

"The character of Choco, has a myriad of shades which one can easily relate with. Her responsibilities as the eldest daughter of the family, her emptiness, her dilemma and her emotional turmoil, all have been wonderfully portrayed."

"The influx of culture is amazingly pleasing. What this author seems to have is a great knack for creating down-to-earth-believable-characters, the kind readers tend to invest serious time in, losing themselves in the characters' problems and struggles. They are not perfect, yet I end up loving them because their imperfections make me cheer them on to victory."

"This is one fun roller coaster of a ride. I totally loved this author's quirky voice, sassy characters and sports references. Choco has such a smart mouth and it was interesting being in her head."

Roaring Hot!

"The characters really pulled on my heart from the very beginning."

"My heart gets so invested in her characters that I just have to see them through to the end."

"The chemistry between Amy and Teo was off the charts!"

"I kinda dislike Amy at first she redeemed herself towards the end ... But Teo I LOVE HIM!!!"

Romance In A Month is a method of writing a romance novel with the help of a community of writers. Our goal is to finish a single plotline romance in a month of writing time.

Learn the basics of writing a romance, characterization, plot points, motivation and goals, and how to speed up your writing by using common romance tropes and archetypes. Exercises, slides, and examples are also included to guide you in creating your own unique romance.

Form your own group of writers to encourage and pace each other. There's strength in numbers, and this guide book will show you how to successfully and consistently write along with a group.

An appendix of romance writing resources includes: tropes, events, roles, occupations, how to brainstorm titles, a reading list by trope.

So start your romance writing journey today with this must-have resource guide to write a romance in thirty days.

About the Author

Rachelle Ayala is a bestselling Asian American author of dramatic romantic suspense and humorous, sexy contemporary romances. Her heroines are feisty and her heroes hot. She writes emotionally challenging stories but believes in the power of love and hope.

Rachelle is the founder of an online writing group, Romance in a Month, an active member of the California Writer's Club, Fremont Chapter, and a volunteer for the World Literary Cafe. She is a very happy woman and lives in California with her husband. She has won awards in multicultural and historical romance.

Check out her website at http://rachelleayala.me and find her books at online retailers Amazon, Barnes and Noble, Kobo, Apple iBookstore, and more.

Fiction: *Michal's Window, Broken Build, Hidden Under Her Heart, Chance for Love Boxed Set, Knowing Vera, Taming Romeo, Whole Latte Love, Played by Love, Playing the Rookie, A Father for Christmas, Claiming Carlos, Roaring Hot!, Love is Easy, Christmas Flirt*

Nonfiction: *Your Daily Bible Verse, Romance in a Month, 366 Ways to Know Your Character*

Made in the USA
San Bernardino, CA
21 June 2015